The Spanish Attraction

The British Presence in Spain from 1830 to 1965

Simon Grayson

Photograph and picture acknowledgements

Anabel Davies collection, London...Page 90.
Residencia de Estudiantes, Madrid ......Pages 74–79.
Archivo General de la Administración, Alcalá de Henares...
     Pages 72 (Upper and lower photos) , 73, 92–95, 104, 108, 109.
Biblioteca Nacional, Madrid.........Pages 14, 15 (Upper and lower
     photos), 16,18–22, 25, 88, 100.
Palacio Real (Patrimonio Nacional), Madrid...Pages 24–26 , 68–71.
Arxiu Autoritat Portuària de Barcelona ...Pages 102–103 (Upper
     and lower photos).
Archivo del Puerto de Bilbao..........Page 29.
Archivo Foral de Bizkaia, Bilbao ....Pages 28, 30, 3.
Athletic Club, Bilbao......Pages 64–67.
Sociedad Bilbaina, Bilbao.......Page 32.
Archivo Bestard, Mallorca............Pages 106–107.
Garrison Library, Gibraltar......Pages 56–60.
Archivo Febles, Tenerife.........Pages 36–41, 105.
Archivo Histórico González Byass.....Pages 33–35.
Fundación Rio-Tinto...Pages 42–55, 62.
National Portrait Gallery, London.....Page 12.
University College London - George Orwell Collection.....Page 91.
Laurie Lee Estate (Mrs. Laurie Lee) ....Page 85.
Gerald Brenan archives....Pages 82–83.
Hotel Eldorado collection, Carboneras, Almeria....Page 96.
Source unknown...Page 86.

Photographers

Wayne Chasan....Page 61.
Bengt Adin.....Pages 80.
David Baird....Page 84.
Michael Lewin...Pages 98–99.

The Spanish Attraction

is published by:

Ediciones Santana S.L.,

Apartado 422, 29640 Fuengirola (Málaga), Spain.

Tel 952 485 838. Fax 952 485 367.

E-mail santana@vnet.es

First published in 2001.
Copyright © Simon Grayson

Edited by David Mitchell

Design and typesetting by John Harper.
Cover design by Tina Bradley

Imprime: Gráficas San Pancracio, S.L.
Polígono Industrial San Luis, calle Orotava, 17, Málaga, Spain.

Depósito Legal: MA-1.394/2001   ISBN: 84-89954-19-4

Simon Grayson was born in Oxford, England, and has lived in Spain for more than ten years. He is a graduate of political science from Warwick University. In 1992 he set up one of the first professional stock shot film libraries in Spain and has worked as a film and photography researcher on numerous projects – a CD-Rom on the history of 20th century Spain for the Spanish Ministry of Culture and a photography exhibition on science for the Fundación Telefónica. He is married and lives in Madrid.

Acknowledgements

My sincerest thanks to Andrew Moore of the British Hispanic Foundation for his enthusiastic support for the project, Theresa Querajazu of the Camara de Comercio de Bilbao for her help and contacts.

Thanks also to Derek Doyle, British Vice-Consul in Bilbao for his practical advice, Louise Highham of the British Council Barcelona, Helen Watson, British Vice-Consul Ibiza, Patrick Campbell of the British Consulate in Alicante, J.L. Blakemore British Consul in Palma de Mallorca, Modesto Piñeiro, British Consul Santander and Barbara M. Payes of the British Consulate in Las Palmas and Lorna Swift of the Garrison Library, Gibraltar.

To my friends:

Many thanks to Ted and Mercedes for driving me down to "Rio Tinto", John McCloskey for sorting out some of the problems in London, Martin Davis (Ibiza) for his invaluable advice and suggestions, Maria José Mulet (Baleares) for her contacts, Chelo and José Vicente for their hospitality while we were in Bilbao, Carlos Casaseca for his generosity and kindness in Barcelona, Heather Hughes for her excellent technical advice, Trinidad Manso for her help with typing the manuscript and Ronald Watson for his friendship and encouragement.

Dedication – To Maite my wife, with all my love.

Contents

Chapter I	Handbook and Bible	13
Chapter II	Through Welsh Eyes	17
Chapter III	Boats, Bananas, Sherry and the Stars	23
Chapter IV	Riotinto	43
Chapter V	Tally Ho!	57
Chapter VI	A Game of Ball	63
Chapter VII	Victoria Eugenia	69
Chapter VIII	Illustrious Visitors	75
Chapter IX	The Spanish Attraction	81
Chapter X	The Idealists	87
Chapter XI	Sir Alexander Fleming	93
Chapter XII	David Lean	97
Chapter XIII	A Genteel Invasion	101

FOREWORD
by David Mitchell

Spain, the land and its people, has probably been more closely observed and anatomised than any other country in Europe. And I think it is fair to say that the English, or less narrowly the British, have more persistently felt and voluminously expressed the Spanish Attraction than any other visitors.

"The very name of Spain awakens in the mind ideas of something romantic and uncommon", wrote Alexander Jardine, British consul at La Coruna in the 1780s. Compared to France, Spain had "more of pure nature, sincerity and sound sense". Its ruins – "so many old castles, towns and mansions, the sad remains of former grandeur" – appealed to the imagination, as did the rugged sierras, equally rugged peasants, and the fact that ways of life, elsewhere dead or dying, were still flourishing

Commenting on Spain's slide from imperial glory into picturesque decay, Jardine argued that the influence of such natural barriers as mountain chains and rivers on linguistic and cultural differences made centralised rule both unworkable and undesirable. Long administrative delays and stubborn local resistance to decrees from Madrid had, in his view, created chaos, cynicism and a truculent *individualismo*.

He noted that foreign visitors were likely to be torn between an urge to "improve" Spain and delight in its unreconstructed backwardness. They could feel superior, or wallow in antiquarian nostalgia, or both.

In the later 18th century upper class English travellers began to put Spain on the cultural tourist map, until then mostly confined to France and Italy. In the 19th century Richard Ford's massive but immensely readable *Handbook for Travellers in Spain* and the self-glorifying evangelist George Borrow's *The Bible in Spain*, still classics of their kind, encouraged the first stirrings of package tourism at about the same time as their French counterparts, Alexandre Dumas and Theophile Gautier. They were the harbingers of a remarkable line of British hispanophiles, stretching from Havelock Ellis to V.S. Pritchett, Gerald Brenan, Robert Graves and Laurie Lee, not to forget such doughty female travel writers as Matilda Betham-Edwards and John Betjeman's wife, Penelope Chetwode.

But British interest and influence was not just literary. British commercial activity in Spain began in the 14th century, when English wine merchants established themselves in the sherry or "sack" producing areas of Andalucía, and later shipped sack from the Canary Islands. Geoffrey Chaucer, son of a vintner, refers to "the fumositee" (fortified strength) of "this wine from Spain" in The Canterbury Tales.

By the 1530s these merchants had formed the Andalusia Company, or Brotherhood of St George, and survived much harassment during the long conflict with heretical England. Sir Francis Drake's devastating raid on Cádiz in 1587 made him a local ogre and mothers to this day are said to scare their children with the threat that "El Draque will get you if you are not good". Among Drake's plunder was a vast quantity of sack, much of it taken from ships preparing for the Armada's invasion of England.

By the 1870s the British, or rather Anglo-Spanish, "Lords of Jerez", now producing brandy as well as sherry, were supplying more than 40 percent of Great Britain's total wine imports, and were noted for their characteristically English clothes and aristocratic lifestyle.

A group of imposing Sherry Barons is immortalised in one of the photographs which Simon Grayson has selected from little explored archives. Here, too, are examples of the photographer Charles Clifford's extensive mid-19th century coverage of the historical monuments of Spain and of major civil engineering projects that initiated the country's late-coming modernisation. As this gathered pace, Spain was studded with British industrial colonies, including shipbuilders in Bilbao and Cadiz, port-builders and banana and tomato cultivators in the Canaries. Railway construction offered another outlet for British capital, machinery and expertise, and around all these operations grew banks, suburbs, shops and clannish clubhouses.

Nowhere was the Raj-like, class-conscious mentality so extreme as at the spectacular British-led Riotinto mining complex near Huelva, where intermarriage with the locals was taboo, and the strictly disciplined Spanish workers were provided with "civilising" schools as an act of missionary *noblesse oblige.* Sport, too, was well catered for and Riotinto was probably the birthplace of the Spanish passion for football, for a while dominated by British coaches and players, notably at the famous Basque club Athletic Bilbao.

It is curious to reflect that the English academic ideal of balancing intellectual and sporting activity – the Oxford and Cambridge ethos – heavily influenced the curriculum of the Residencia de Estudiantes in Madrid, where such unconventional types as Salvador Dalí and García Lorca were students in the 1920s. At that time the fashion-conscious, English-born Queen Victoria Eugenia, consort of the erratic King Alfonso XIII, succeeded in changing the sombre sartorial ways of the Spanish court. And the Royal Calpe Hunt, founded in 1813 and based in Gibraltar, was at the peak of its Anglo-Spanish splendour, soon to fade as civil war loomed after the King and Queen went into exile in 1931.

In the plangently evocative Riotinto and Calpe Hunt photographs one senses that indeed, as the saying goes, "the past is another country". British idealism and eccentricity still, however, flourished during the Civil War, strikingly so in the figure of George Orwell, whose libertarian instincts accorded so well with the passionate sentiments of Spanish anarchists and dissident Marxists.

Two British heroes who received triumphal tributes in Spain during the Franco regime were Sir Alexander Fleming, the discoverer of penicillin, and a maverick warrior chieftain idealised in the movie *Lawrence of Arabia*. Directed by the Englishman David Lean, this epic undertaking, partly located in Spain, made Almería for some years a favourite region for film-makers, particularly those specialising in westerns.

Simon Grayson offers some final telling images of the impetus given to the tourist industry by British enterprise, moving in about 70 years from genteel wintering in Málaga or Gran Canaria to modern-day package tourism that wrought a social, moral and commercial revolution on the Costas.

Has the impact of mass tourism, so distasteful to Brenan, Graves and Laurie Lee, obliterated the picturesque, many-faceted "difference" that was once the essence of the Spanish Attraction? Or have some vestiges survived? The jury is still out on that one.

Chapter I
Handbook and Bible
Richard Ford and George Borrow

Even after the defeat of the Armada in 1588 Spain, though now a shaky super power, was still England's prime enemy. Attitudes were already changing when, in the 18th century, some enterprising Englishmen, notably Henry Swinburne and Richard Twist, began to put Spain on the cultural tourist map, a process continued by diplomats and British army officers during the Peninsular War (1809-1814).

But the first real attempt at a comprehensive account was provided by Richard Ford in his celebrated *Handbook for Travellers in Spain* (1845) and its handier companion *Gatherings from Spain* (1846). Sometimes accompanied by his wife Harriet, this rich Tory patrician, setting out from a base in Seville, criss-crossed Spain from end to end on horseback, riding over mule tracks "with ruts as deep as ancient prejudices."

The result of these strenuous tours, undertaken from 1830 to 1833, was the *Handbook*. Compiled in England with the help of a Spanish correspondent, Don Pascual de Gayangos, it was a hefty, expensive work with more than 1000 closely printed pages of text, 140 itineraries and a 50-page index. Yet the racy style and pungent opinions turned it and *Gatherings* into bestsellers of their genre.

Ford saw Spain, so gloriously backward, as "a land bottled up for antiquarians", where smuggling was the only efficiently organised industry, and government was a chaotic bureaucracy presiding over a population which, due to a long Moorish occupation, "hovers between Europe and Africa, between the hat and the turban." Unlike some British travellers, he found the bullfight an exciting spectacle, "as the brilliant army of combatants separate like a bursting shell and take up their respective places as regularly as our fielders at a cricket match."

The many sketches and etchings made by the Fords are often the only record of buildings and localities vanished or changed beyond recognition, while the evocative engravings of the Alhambra in Granada by David Wilkie projected a powerful image of romantic, ruinous Spain. With its Moorish/African aspects, Andalucía became a favourite venue for other "exotic" artists, such as David Roberts.

In that other bestseller *The Bible in Spain* (1843), the eccentric, bombastic Protestant mis-

Facing page: Richard Ford, the great chronicler of nineteenth century Spain. His "Handbook for Traveller's in Spain (1845)" was the classic forerunner to the modern guide book.

sionary George Borrow, with his interest in gypsies and admiration for Moorish culture, also helped to focus attention on Andalucía as the most picturesque region of Spain. Seville, he wrote "is a magic scene...I have shed tears of rapture while I beheld it".

Between them, Ford and Borrow helped to ensure that the abundant folk cultures they relished would be eroded by train-borne tourism. For Thomas Cook and other pioneering tour operators, Seville and Granada were the main destinations. Ford lamented that "the relentless march of European intellect is crushing many a native wildflower".

By the 1860s, in *Cosas de España*, one of the first female British travel writers, Mrs W.P. Byrne, prayed that the inevitable impacts of industrial revolution would not be too devastating, that somehow Spain "would escape the blasting breath

of the Iron Age unscathed." And in the 1890s the sociologist Havelock Ellis described the tourist invasion as resembling a plague of locusts nibbling away at the roots of cultures already under threat from progressively minded Spaniards.

Facing page: Sir David Wilkie, the nineteenth century Scottish artist who immortalised Spain´s monuments and people in paintings and engravings. *Above*: his engravings of "The Spanish Lady" and "The Duke of Wellington sending despatches."

Chapter II

Through Welsh Eyes
Royal Photographer Charles Clifford

The Welsh-born photographer Charles Clifford and the Frenchman Jean Laurent were the great chroniclers of Spain in the 19th century. Their extraordinary photographs of the monuments, people, customs and construction projects of that time are now considered a national treasure.

Soon after meeting Clifford in the Alhambra of Granada, the Danish writer Hans Christian Andersen wrote: "On the orders of Her Majesty the Queen, the Patio de los Leones and the Sala de las Hermanas were being photographed by a famous English photographer…nobody was allowed to enter for fear of interrupting his work."

Charles Clifford was extremely versatile — a mixture of artist, scientist and adventurer. He was an enthusiastic aeronaut in hot-air balloons as well as a gifted photographer who introduced to Spain the latest techniques from abroad.

These qualities, combined with a keen business sense, prompted him to embark on his most ambitious project. From 1850, having established a studio in Madrid where he was a successful portrait photographer (using the original copper-plated daguerreotypes), he spent many years travelling the length and breadth of the country taking photographs.

These were then put together in albums and entitled Journey to Valladolid (1858), Journey to Alicante, the Balearic Islands and Barcelona (1860), Journey to the Provinces of Toledo and Extremadura (1858), and Journey to Andalucía and Murcia (1862). These albums constitute one of the most important photographic records of that time. Such was Clifford's success that Queen Victoria and other European Monarchs commissioned him to compile other comprehensive coverages of Spanish cities and monuments.

In 1858, Clifford's career was greatly boosted when he was appointed Court Photographer to Queen Isabel II, an honour indeed for a foreigner. In Spain at that time, photography was still very much in its infancy and the Queen's advisers recognised its potential to promote the image and importance of the monarchy to the widest possible public. Probably, Clifford's most distinguished documentary work was his coverage of the Canal Isabel II, an epic depiction of an engineering project that involved hundreds of workers build-

Facing page:
The "Patio de los Leones" in the Alhambra, Granada, photographed in 1862 by Charles Clifford, official photographer to the Court of Queen Isabel II.

ing the pipelines and aqueducts to supply water to Madrid.

When Clifford died in 1863, his wife Jane, for long a capable assistant, took over the flourishing business. Her photographic documentation of the treasures of the Royal Collection can be seen in the archives of the Royal Palace, Madrid.

In a short lifetime, Clifford's energy and output were prodigious. Yet despite his fame, nothing is known of his early years, the exact date and place of his birth being apparently unrecorded. There are even conflicting versions of his

Facing page: the wharf arch in Cádiz, just one of the 800 and some photographs of monuments and palaces in the Charles Clifford collection that forms a significant part of Spain's national heritage. *Above:* some villagers pose for Clifford in Ibiza.

Above and facing page: two of the many spectacular photographs taken by Clifford in 1855 and 1856 of the construction of the Canal Isabel II.

career in Spain. Some experts say that he was not Court Photographer to Isabel II, but was essentially a protégé of Queen Victoria, commissioned to work mainly in Spain. What is certain is that his work brilliantly complements the Spanish sketches, paintings and prints of David Wilkie, David Roberts and the Fords.

Most of Charles Clifford's photographs can be found in the *Biblioteca Nacional*, Madrid.

Chapter III

Boats, Bananas, Sherry and the Stars
British Industry and Technology in 19th century Spain

In the 19th century, British industrial and commercial involvement with Spain was largely confined to the major ports and to areas where primary materials were exploited.

In the north, British mining and shipbuilding interests were located in Bilbao. In the northeast, rapidly increasingly industrial development in Catalonia offered great opportunities for capital investment and a wide range of specialised machinery, notably in Barcelona, known as "the Manchester of Spain" for its flourishing textile factories. Barcelona was also a busy port catering for tourists on cruise ships and liners.

In the south, Andalucía was particularly attractive to British enterprise: the port of Cádiz for shipbuilders and wine exporters, the port of Huelva for transporting minerals extracted from the British-owned Riotinto mines, and Jerez de la Frontera where the famous Anglo-Spanish sherry producing families established their bodegas.

In the Canary Islands, British capital and expertise was especially prominent; so much so that in 1887, in *Tenerife and its Six Satellites*, Olivia Stone reported that "the businesses are principally in English hands."

Coaling depots for British shipping en route to West and South Africa and beyond were established in Las Palmas and Santa Cruz. The surrounding shipyards were British-owned; and in other major construction projects British engineers played a crucial role in the construction of railways and roads. The construction of the Isabel II railway in the north of Spain is documented in a series of photographs by the British engineer William Atkinson.

Bananas, tomatoes, potatoes, oranges, almonds and pulses were exported to Britain, while British textiles, steel and machinery were imported. By 1902 nearly 1,400 British ships docked at Puerto de la Luz. Banking and insurance facilities were expanded.

The Canaries were successfully promoted as highly desirable health resorts for well-to-do Victorians. Hotels, many of them British-owned, multiplied in Gran Canaria and Tenerife; and in Las Palmas a garden city was built for British residents. This increased clientele generated shopping streets (selling British goods), bars, restaurants and even photographic studios, all mainly British-owned.

Facing page: the Sheepshanks telescope erected on Mount Guajara in Tenerife in 1857 by Scottish astronomer Charles Piazzi Smyth.

Above: the locomotive Isabel II, photographed in 1855 by William Atkinson (*facing page*), the British engineer in charge of the Isabel II Railway.

In Tenerife in 1857, Mount Guajara, 2,717 metres above sea level, was the location of a remarkable scientific experiment by the Scottish astronomer Charles Piazzi Smyth. In his *Tenerife: an Astronomer's Experiment*, Smyth successfully demonstrated Isaac Newton's hypothesis that telescopes, in order to obtain maximum visibility, should be placed at a high altitude. Smyth himself recorded his experiment in a series of photographs now housed in the *Biblioteca Nacional* in Madrid.

The Basque Connection

The history of the Basque Port of Bilbao is to a very large extent the history of the Ría, the narrow estuary of the river Nervion that flows through the city on its way to the Bay of Biscay.

Since the Middle Ages, ships have sailed back and forth through its murky, treacherous waters laden with cargoes of every description and size, including wool, wine, corn, flour, iron ore and machinery. The city owes its prosperity and its progressive, cosmopolitan culture to the Ría.

Facing page: Alfred S. Jee, Chief Engineer of the Isabel II Railway project, who died on the job in Caldas just before the line was inaugurated in August 1858. *Above:* a ship being built in 1918 by the British company Clark & Standfield in the Cádiz shipyards.

Bilbao and the province of Vizcaya have enjoyed a close commercial relationship with Britain since the 15th century when, in 1474, King Edward IV signed a trade agreement allowing Vizcayan merchants to trade in England. In the same year, in the town of Guernica, a similar agreement was signed giving English merchants the right to trade in the province of Vizcaya.

In the second half of the 19th century, Bilbao became well known for its iron and steel industry. British companies such as the Bilbao River & Cantabrian Railway, the Orconera Iron Ore Co. Ltd, and Luchana Mining were among the numerous foreign companies that exploited the rich iron ore reserves of the region.

Facing page: an engraving of the launching of the "Vizcaya Cruiser" that was built with the help of British engineers. *Above:* ships of the British-owned Orconera Iron Ore company and the Luchana Mining Company docked in the Ría of Bilbao in 1909.

Above: women unloading a ship on the banks of the Ría in Bilbao in 1884 in a spot known as "The English meadow" because so many British ships docked there.

In a constant flow of cargo steamers between the UK and Bilbao, British coke was imported and used to fire up the furnaces of the iron and steel mills of the famous Altos Hornos de Vizcaya. The iron ingots were then shipped to Britain to be turned into steel.

At that time, Britain was also much involved in the shipbuilding industry in Bilbao. In 1889, a British construction company owned by Sir Charles Palmer set up the Astilleros Nervión

(the Nervion shipyards) where three battleships were built for the Spanish navy. The John K. Moffat shipyard was also active in shipbuilding and repairs.

Bilbao is very much a city of the north, its climate being closer to that of Liverpool than to that of Cádiz or Tarragona. Being a port, it has always been open to cultural and political influences from other countries. The British influence can be seen in some of the solid Victorian-style

Above: a photograph taken in 1894 of the British-owned Oronera Iron Ore Company mines in Bilbao.

Above: the "English Bar" of the exclusive Sociedad Bilbaina that was the traditional meeting place for British industrialists and residents in Bilbao.

architecture and in the Sociedad Bilbaina, the prestigious club in calle Navarra where the Gibraltar Room used to be the meeting place for British industrialists and expatriates living in Bilbao.

The football team Athletic Club is spelt the English way, rather than the Spanish Atletico, in recognition of the English players and managers of the beginning of the century. And the city has one of the most modern underground systems in the world, designed by the British architect Norman Foster.

The Lords of Jerez

Sir Alexander Fleming once said: "If penicillin can cure those that are ill, Spanish sherry can bring the dead back to life!"

Jerez de la Frontera became world famous for the production of its fortified wines, named after the town, which the British pronounced as "sherry". Originally the town stood on the border between the Moorish and the Christian kingdoms, hence the name Jerez de la Frontera.

The towns of Jerez, Sanlúcar de Barrameda and Puerto de Santa María in south west

Above: the Gilbey family, photographed in the Royal Bodega de la Concha of González Byass in 1883.

Andalucía form the "Golden Triangle" of vineyards and bodegas where sherry and brandy are produced. The climate in that part of Spain is ideal for making sweet wines, since the blazing sun- of Andalucía ripens the grapes with a high sugar content that gives sherry its distinctive flavour.

Since the 18th century, the production of sherry and, later on, of brandy has been dominated by a number of families whose names can be seen over the doors of bodegas throughout the area, names such as Harvey, Domecq, González-Byass, Terry and Osborne. As can be seen from their surnames, these families have their origins in various countries: Harvey, Osborne and Byass are of English descent, the Terrys are of Irish ancestry and the Domecqs are from France.

Sherry was popularised in Britain around 1855 by Robert Blake Byass, a British wine merchant who went into business with the Spanish entrepreneur Manuel González. A former bank employee, González had ploughed all his savings and a loan from his Uncle Pepe – later to be honoured as Tío Pepe, the name given to the famous dry sherry – into the bodega that was to feature the famous González-Byass trademark. The González family still control the business.

The Osborne family is descended from Thomas Osborne, an Englishman from Exeter who, with a little help from his friend the British Consul, set up his bodega in Cádiz in 1772. He later moved the bodega to Puerto de Santa María and married the daughter of a well-known local wine merchant. From these beginnings sprang the Osborne dynasty.

The Terry family arrived in Puerto de Santa María in the 1850s. Brilliant entrepreneurs, it was not long before they had married into the most important Spanish and Italian families involved in the wine trade. The 'golden years' of the family business lasted until the 1970s, when a crisis in the sherry and brandy industry forced them to sell out to a multinational company. Today, the Osborne and González-Byass bodegas are the only surviving family-run businesses.

Facing page: John David Gordon (1774-1850), a British wine merchant based in Jerez de la Frontera. *Above:* Mercedes Cristina Gilbey Gordon, who married Ricardo L. González in London in 1923 and died in Jerez.

The Fortunate Islands

The first book by an Englishman on the Canary Islands, published in 1564 by Thomas Nichols a sugar merchant, was entitled *"A pleasant description of the Fortunate Islands, called the Islands of Canaria with their strange fruits and commodities, very delectable to read to the praise of God."*

Shakespeare refers to wine from the Canaries in three of his plays, *Henry IV*, *The Merry Wives of Windsor* and *Twelfth Night*. As early as 1519, merchant ships from Bristol were anchored offshore to transport wine known as Sack or Canary to taverns and households in England.

In the 19th century, Anglo-Canarian commerce was greatly expanded when coaling stations were established to refuel merchant ships from London or Liverpool on long-haul voyages. By the 1850s, British companies virtually monopolised all the activities in the ports of Las Palmas and Tenerife. The construction of La Luz Port, began in 1883 by Swanston & Company, accelerated this process.

By 1900, British households were stocking up on bananas, tomatoes, potatoes, almonds, oranges and tobacco from the Canary Islands, while the islanders, many of whom worked for British businesses, were able to buy such British products as cigarettes, beer, cotton, Lifebuoy toilet soap, biscuits, cough mixture and perfumes.

The establishment of the telegraph in 1883, together with improvements to communications and tranport, marked the beginnings of a tourism boom and the Canary Islands soon became a

Left: bananas being piled up in the British-owned Yeoward Company yard in Tenerife, ready for loading onto ships bound for England.

favourite holiday destination for the burgeoning British middle-classes, attracted by " the peace and tranquillity and the perfect climate." The medicinal qualities of the local mineral waters were endlessly debated in the British press and the medical journals of the time. In fact, the vast majority of the early British visitors were convalescents rather than sun-seeking tourists.

This constant flow of visitors to the Islands provided an ideal opportunity for the British residents, many of whom were living in the famous

Facing page: the T.M. Reid company that exported vegetables and was owned by the British Vice Consul in Tenerife. *Above*: Parson Andrews, his wife, their dog and the donkey he rode when visiting his parishioners in Tenerife.

Above: British residents in Tenerife celebrating Edward VII´s ascension to the throne in 1901.
Facing page: a patriotic British resident during carnival time in Tenerife around 1905.

Garden City in Las Palmas, to set up tourism-related businesses such as shops, bars, restaurants, banks and hotels. Names such as the Orotava Grand Hotel, Camacho´s Hotel, Taoro Grand Hotel, Bellavista Hotel, Santa Catalina Hotel and the Metropole Hotel in Gran Canaria are a part of the story of the British involvement in the Canary Islands.

Today, the anglicisms still to be heard in the language spoken by Canarians — for instance, *queque* (cake) *naife* or *nife* (knife), *pudin* (pudding) and *moni* (money) — bear witness to British influence on the islands.

Chapter IV

Riotinto

The Legendary Mines in Huelva

British merchants, settled in Andalucía since the 14th century, have left a lingering trace in what might now be called elitist customs. The ferias of Seville and Jerez feature marquees resembling those of an English garden party, exclusive enclosures where the real patrician arrives on horseback. In Jerez, the "sherry barons" created a clubbish culture dominated by English social manners and tailoring, so that the city is still widely regarded as the quintessential home of the senorito or "toff".

But nowhere in Spain did the British leave such a spectacular physical, social and architectural legacy as at the Riotinto mining complex. The Phoenicians and Romans first exploited what may be the world's oldest worked mines. Spaniards reopened them in 1724, but not until a British-led international consortium bought them in 1873 were they exploited on a massive scale.

From Pozo Alfredo, a 2000-foot-deep cut, came copper; from the Colorado cut, copper, silver and gold, from elsewhere iron pyrites. Still today, Corte Atalaya, Europe's largest open mine, a huge crater with stepped sides dwarfing an acid-red lake, is an awesome sight — a man-made Grand Canyon in the middle of Huelva province.

By the 1880s, the Riotinto Company controlled an operation which employed 10,000 workers, some from as far afield as Asturias and Galicia, with 130 locomotives transporting the minerals to the port of Huelva.

The engineering and managerial staff were predominantly British, and a form of apartheid similar to that of the Indian Raj was gradually imposed. The introduction of football was good for worker morale and the educational, medical and housing facilities at Riotinto were envied by industrial workers in other parts of Spain, but other developments, culminating in the strike of 1888 which ended in tragedy when government troops opened fire on the unarmed workers who had marched on the company offices in protest at the devastating effects of the pollution caused by the mineral mounds, did not improve industrial relations.

The British community, known as "La Colonia Inglesa", lived separately from the locals. Bella Vista, a hilltop estate of Victorian-style villas, included an imposing clubhouse and a neo-Gothic

Facing page: miners and engineers at the work face of the legendary Riotinto copper mine in Huelva, and the mounds where minerals were burnt, creating a dense blanket of toxic fumes that sometimes forced the villagers to evacuate their homes and flee to the fresh air of the surrounding hills.

Above: Gordon Douglas, supervising engineer at the Corte Atalaya mine face. *Facing page*: the demolition of a church to make way for new mining works.

Protestant chapel in which the Archdeacon of Gibraltar took communion service each Sunday, and the estate was protected by closely guarded gates.

By contrast with Jerez de la Frontera, where intermarriage produced an Anglo-Spanish aristocracy, the British at Riotinto were discouraged from marrying Spanish women, and if they disobeyed this unwritten rule they were expelled from the Colony. Though this ban was lifted in

the 1920s, the same attitude persisted. Spanish brides were accepted but had to follow the code of the Colony.

This included such un-Spanish rituals and pastimes as the cult of Santa Claus, the non-operation of the British-built railway line to Huelva on Queen Victoria's birthday (also commemorated by an egg-and-spoon race), croquet, amateur dramatics and a Ladies Only afternoon tea party in the clubhouse on Wednesdays. There were lawn tennis courts, walled gardens and tree-lined avenues, and a hard-won Bella Vista connection increased one's standing in Huelvan society.

Lesser employees were housed in Huelva's Barrio Reina Victoria, built in the early 1900s. The neat, cream coloured terraces are now sometimes painted more vividly. But until quite recently a few of the houses in this enclave of English suburbia, dwarfed by towering apartment blocks, were occupied by retired company employees, or their relatives, paying peppercorn rents for a desirable residence with ornamental gable ends and chimney pots. At the nearby coastal resort of Punta Umbría, a few of the half-timbered Riotinto Company's holiday bungalows are still to be seen.

The mines, which Franco, irritated by their foreign ownership, often referred to as "an economic Gibraltar", were bought back in 1954 and the last British employees left in the 1970s. Today, with mineral riches virtually exhausted, a Riotinto Foundation is in the process of turning the whole complex into an industrial theme park,

Left: inside the Riotinto foundry. At the height of its power, the company employed over 10,000 people.

Above: The Riotinto store that sold a wide range of imported British products. *Facing page*: a residential street in the mining town that looked more Victorian than Andalusian.

with a historical museum in abandoned warehouses. The Edwardian headquarters building, though semi-ruinous, has the ticket windows where, as decreed by the Company, pay-day wages were collected by miners' wives lest their husbands should drink most of it away in bars.

Describing a visit to Bella Vista in the early 1990s, Michael Jacobs called it "a presence as incongruous in the Andalusian countryside as a white Andalusian hill village would have been in the middle of Surrey...the one concession to local taste being the use of stone rather than brick."

The residents are now mostly doctors and their families from a large new hospital in the vicinity. The neo-Gothic chapel is a popular background for wedding photographs, and the clubhouse remains central to the social scene of a hispanicised colony which nevertheless keeps some British traditions – a Men Only Bar, Ladies Only teas on Wednesdays, worn leather armchairs, hunting scenes on the walls and sporting trophies on shelves.

Bella Vista still has social cachet, not least as represented, until recently, by "Mr Green" – real

Facing page: the families of the British engineers and managers playing tennis. *Above:* British children competing in an egg -and-spoon race on sports day at Riotinto

name Pablo Verde – who had worked in the British Club since the 1940s. He remembered the concerts and Gilbert and Sullivan operettas. He would tell how, when carrying a tray of drinks to the billiard room, he dutifully waited until the click of ball on ball signalled that he could enter without disturbing a member's concentration, and he took pride in showing resplendent WCs with mahogany seats and ceramic bowls displaying an English cottage motif surrounded by the words "J. F. Hutton and Co., Purveyors of Luxury Sanitary Furnishings to the Late Queen Victoria."

Facing page: the memorial to British "members of the staff at Riotinto Mines who fell in the Great War of 1914-1919." *Above:* the school for the mine and rail workers´ children.

Above: children of the British community with members of the Guardia Civil. *Facing page*: Franco shakes hands with one of the British managers of Riotinto after the mines had been sold back to Spain.

The Men Only bar had relaxed its rules in the sixties and allowed members to bring their wives if they paid a fine in the form of a bottle of whiskey "so that other members could drink to their health." This quaint custom went well for a while until three doctors from the Riotinto hospital refused to pay the fine on the grounds that the men-only rule was macho and anachronistic. On being expelled from the club as rebels, the doctors took their case to the local courts and won a sentence from a judge in Huelva that ruled the Club must open its Men Only doors to women.

Chapter V

Tally Ho!

The Royal Calpe Hunt

In the 1870s, the Rev. H. J. Rose, Chaplain to the British Communities at Jerez and Cádiz, reported that "one of the brightest signs of real, honest, social advancement in southern Spain is the desertion of the bullring; and the pouring in, like a slow flood, of all sorts of manly exercises…in Cádiz and Seville, in Port Saint Mary and Jerez, and in other cities, horse-racing, boat-racing, and above all cricket matches are now very common…And, let me say, the finest fielders are the Spaniards; their sleight of hand and quickness of eye are the theme of universal admiration. A Spaniard very rarely misses a catch."

There was perhaps a good deal of wishful thinking in his comments, and the Rev. Rose does not mention British sporting influence as seen in the already well established Calpe Hunt, based in Gibraltar. Yet as related in Gordon Fergusson's book "*Hounds are Home*", the Calpe Hunt, which in 1906 became the Royal Calpe Hunt with Edward VII and Alfonso XIII as joint patrons, was a remarkable example of Anglo-Spanish sporting co-operation. For 125 years, a pack of hounds, kennelled on the Rock, pursued foxes, deer, and occasionally wild boar, over nearby Spanish terrain from San Roque and Los Barrios north to Castellar.

Said to have been founded in 1813 by the Rev. Mark Mackereth, chaplain to Prince Edward, Duke of Kent (then Governor of Gibraltar), the Hunt initially operated on the Upper Rock, where foxes then abounded, but was soon in action across the border with English foxhounds shipped to Cádiz. Grateful for British success in ending French military occupation in Spain, the Spanish were not inclined to prevent officers of the Gibraltar garrison from indulging their peculiar pastime over the countryside beyond La Linea.

Though the Calpe was a British hunt, it had to maintain friendly relations with local Spanish landowners and farmers. At first, meets often took place at the Duke of Kent's farm (bought for his French mistress). Except for a few Spanish names, written reports on the hunts could have been describing a run with the hounds in England, one example being the entry "Ran from near Woodcock Covert in five-and-half-mile ring via Fern Valley, Little White House, Bailey's

Facing page: the Calpe Hunt in 1896. Members were residents and military officers based in Gibraltar and the hunts usually took place in the San Roque area.

Bank and Pinar de Bigotas along the Miraflores track to Pablo's Gorse."

Pablo was Pablo Gerónimo Larios, who had been partly educated in England in the 1880s and had hunted in Yorkshire and the Cotswolds. He and his brothers had ridden with the Calpe as young boys and the Larios family were the leading landowners along the coast to Marbella, and therefore useful in settling any problems with farmers.

Though tradition demanded that the Master of the Hunt should be a British officer, Pablo Larios was in 1891 elected and remained in office, with a short interval, until his death in 1938. He it was who, while the Hunt Committee approached Edward VII, secured the patronage of Alfonso XIII. There was great rejoicing when in the same year (1906) King Alfonso married the English Princess Ena, and from then on the crowns of England and Spain figured on the hunt buttons.

Each king had a gorse covert named after him. A photograph of a meet in 1907 shows a mounted field of more than sixty. Since Spain was neutral during the first world war, hunting was unaffected. Indeed when steeplechases took place on the Larios Estate, special excursions were laid on for Gibraltar residents — by steamer to Algeciras, then to Guadacorte by train. But problems loomed after King Alfonso was forced to abdicate in 1931.

Hunting resumed, however, after a brief lull while vengeful republican mobs were destroying churches in Algeciras and La Linea. Pablo Larios,

Members of the Calpe Hunt Staff (1896-1897) from left: Dan Jordan (Whip and Kennel Huntsman), C.Larios (lst Whip), P. Larios (Master and Huntsman), Lieut. H. Brown (2nd Whip), Capt. C. Findlay (Secretary)

now Marqués de Marzales, was forced to resign as Master by the Governor of Gibraltar, General Sir Alexander Godley, who thought that the hunt "was in danger of becoming altogether too Spanish and too civilian an affair". But a threat from King George V to withdraw his patronage unless Larios was reinstated over-rode the Governor's rash decision.

Hunting was temporarily suspended during the Civil War but was resumed in 1937 when, after Málaga was taken by the Nationalists, General Franco gave permission for the Hunt to meet on two days per week. This matter was questioned in the House of Commons by a Labour M.P., who was informed by the Foreign Secretary, Sir Anthony Eden, that the Royal Calpe Hunt's arrangements with Franco were a "purely local affair."

Ironically, the Nationalist victory in the Civil War put an end to the Royal Calpe Hunt when, at the start of the second world war, Hitler planned to capture Gibraltar with Franco's co-operation. The 24 couples of hounds were put down and, after 42 years' employment with the hunt, José Pecino, the kennel huntsman on the Rock, joined his family in Spain.

The Royal Calpe Hunt was no more, but the tradition was carried on in 1978 when Major Peter Hall, a cavalry officer in India who had retired to southern Spain, started the Guadiaro Hunt with a pack of 36 hounds, and the fields and leafy lanes of San Roque and Los Barrios were once again alive with the cries of Tally Ho!

Above: riders and hounds of the Royal Calpe Hunt being ferried across the river at San Roque in 1907. *Facing page*: Major Peter Hall, a cavalry officer who retired to southern Spain and started the Guadiaro Hunt in 1978.

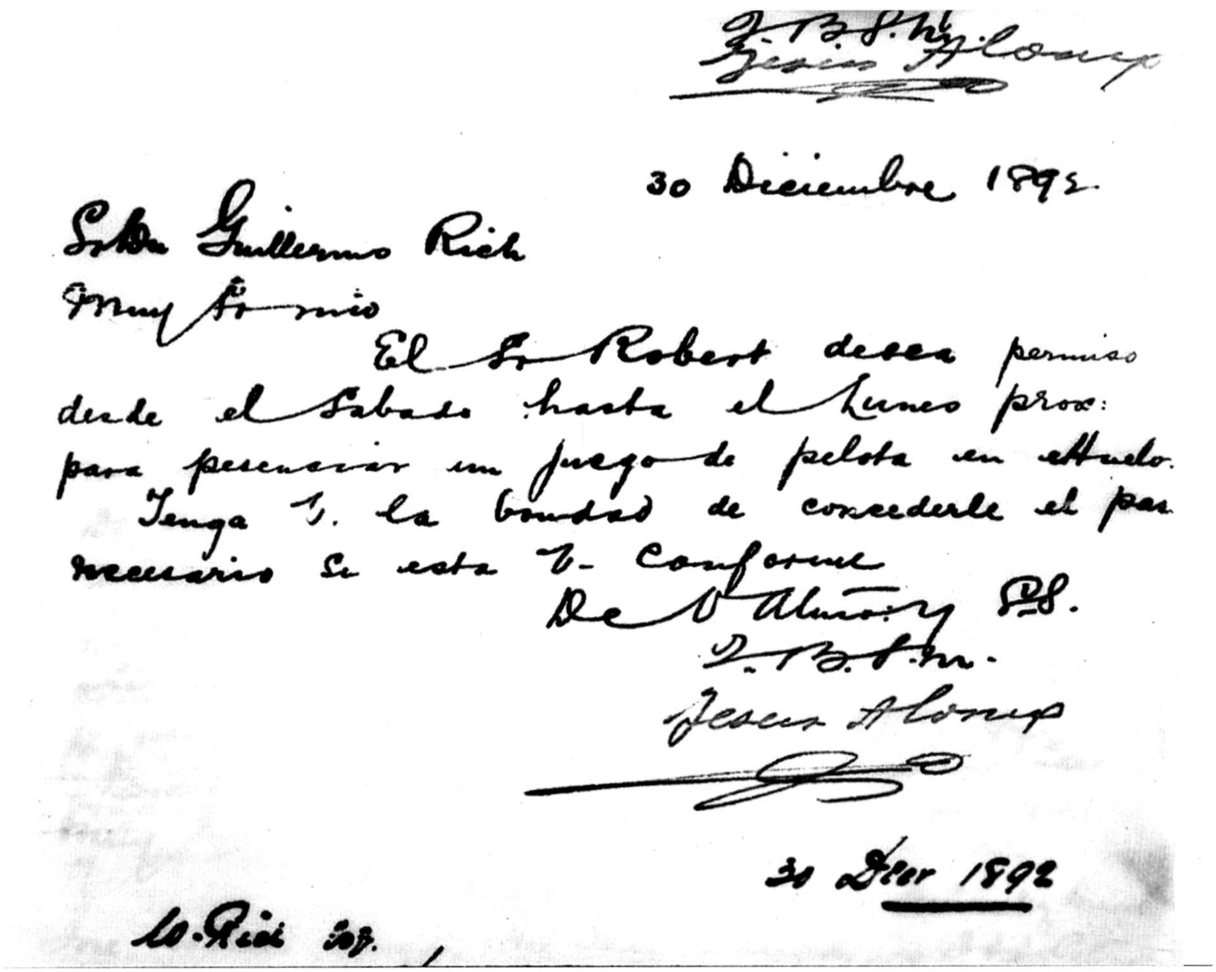

[Handwritten letter in Spanish]

F. B. S. M. Jesús Alonso

30 Diciembre 1892.

Sñor Guillermo Rich

Muy Sr mío

El Sr Robert desea permiso desde el Sábado hasta el Lunes prox: para presenciar un juego de pelota en Huelvo. Tenga V. la bondad de concederle el per necesario si esta V. conforme

De V. afmo y S.S.
F. B. S. M.
Jesús Alonso

30 Dbre 1892

W. Rich Esq.

William Rich
(Managing Director of Riotinto mines)
30 December 1893.

Dear Sir,

Mr. Robert would like permission from Saturday until next Monday to attend a game of ball in Huelva.

If you are in agreement, would you kindly provide him with the necessary pass.

Chapter VI

A Game of Ball

How Soccer Came to Spain

It was 1873, and the locals who lived in the villages near the Riotinto mines had never seen anything like it before. On Saturday mornings, the British engineers would congregate with mine workers in a field to form two groups. In each group were eleven men intent on kicking an inflated leather ball from one end of the field to the other. At either end of the field there were three long sticks that formed a rectangle, and the objective of each group was to kick the ball through the opposing group's rectangle. The game involved a lot of running, jumping, shouting, and occasional hugging and kissing when a "goal" was scored. The game was called "football."

From these beginnings on the dusty fields of Andalucía grew the Huelva Recreation Club which was founded in 1879 – the first football club in Spain. Thus began Spain's passion for "the English game". At that time it was simply called "un juego de pelota" (a ball game), but finally entered the Spanish language as "futbol".

In the port of Bilbao in the mid-1880s, British merchant seamen introduced the Basques to the game. While their ships were being loaded with coal and minerals, the rough-and-ready sailors used to have a kick around to pass the time. Before long the Basque dockers, in spite of being slightly confused about the rules of play, decided to join in.

On 4 May 1894, they challenged the "Robinsones" (the nickname of the English sailors after Daniel Defoe's famous castaway Robinson Crusoe) to a football match, which took place in Lamiaco on the banks of the river Nervion. The home team lost by six goals to five. But this defeat did not dampen the Basques' enthusiasm for the game. In 1898, Juan Astorquia, who had been educated in a Catholic college in Manchester, founded the Athletic Club de Bilbao – the football team that was to become the pride of the Basque Country.

In Barcelona on 29 November 1899, in the Sole Gymnasium on Montjuic, a historic meeting took place between a group of friends led by the Swiss-born Joan Gamper. At this meeting the Football Club of Barcelona – F. C. Barcelona – was officially founded. Its first president was an Englishman called Walter Wild.

Athletic Bilbao, still known by their English name, claim to be the oldest professional or semi-

Facing page: a document dated 30th December 1892 – from the Riotinto mines archive in which an employee asks permission to play a game of ball.

Above: the first photograph taken in 1901 of the original Athletic Club of Bilbao football team that included a number of British players.

professional club, pre-dating Recreativo de Huelva by a few months. A combined Basque team (Athletic and F. C. Vizcaya) were the first winners of the first national competition in 1902, beating Barcelona 2-1. A Spanish referee officiated, but half the Basque team were English, and Parsons, an English player, scored Barcelona's consolation goal.

Perhaps the most important British footballing exports to Spain were the coaches, such as Messrs McKay and Sundheim who founded Recreativo de Huelva, and Fred Pentland, the famous trainer and manager of Athletic Club during the club's golden age from

1925 to 1933. All were referred to as "The Mister", since English surnames tended to be difficult to pronounce, and these tactical wizards were too respected to be addressed by Christian name. Fred Pentland usually wore a bowler hat and suit and smoked cigars but changed to a beret and mackintosh to avoid being recognised when scouting for talent around the local football clubs of Vizcaya.

In recent times, British managers and players on millionaire contracts have experienced mixed fortunes in *"La Liga"* (the Spanish Premiership). Ron Atkinson was sacked by the Atletico Madrid club, and Terry Venables was

Above: the Athletic Club team of 1910 that still had three British players in the side.

Above: the legendary Mr. Pentland, the Athletic Club´s English trainer during its golden age 1925-1933, with two of his players.

summarily dismissed as manager when Barcelona lost to Steaua Buchariest in the final of the European Cup in 1986. These days it's a case of deliver-or-else for "the Mister."

To some extent the same applies to exported British players. Garry Lineker a striker of international standing was much criticised by Barcelona's demanding Dutch manager Johann Cruyff. More recently, Steve McMananan, moving from Liverpool to Real Madrid, has had to compete for a place with even more expensive signings. British players have sometimes had difficulty

getting used to a different culture on and off the field, and in some cases Spaniards moving to England have had the same problem.

The first to make the move, though involuntarily, were Basque refugees from the Civil War, notably Emilio Aldecoa, who played for Wolverhampton Wanderers and Coventry City before returning to his native land. Moving to London from Barcelona for £2.2 million in 1998, Albert Ferrer became a mainstay of Chelsea's Premiership team.

It is all a bewilderingly far cry from the modest beginnings at Riotinto in the 1870s.

Above: Fred Pentland in bowler hat with some members of the Athletic Club team, just after they had beaten the Paris Racing team 5-1 in a friendly match.

Chapter VII

Victoria Eugenia
Spain's English Queen

In her memoirs Eulalia de Borbon, King Alfonso XIII's aunt, wrote "In Windsor there was a beautiful princess, undoubtedly the most beautiful in Europe. She had fair skin, clear eyes, wonderful blonde hair and features that were worthy of a master's hand. She was called Ena of Battenberg and she was the most loved grand-daughter of Queen Victoria."

It was while visiting London in 1905 to meet Edward VII that the young King Alfonso XIII fell hopelessly in love with Edward's niece, Ena Battenberg. She was the daughter of Princess Beatrice and Henry Battenberg and was the first royal child to be born at Balmoral.

A year later, in May 1906, the couple were married in the church of Los Jerónimos in Madrid. But this fairytale wedding ended in tragedy when an Anarchist threw a bomb at the royal wedding carriage. Although the young couple were unhurt, 24 people died in the assassination attempt. Such a beginning did not augur well for the King and Queen as the country entered a period of political turbulence and uncertainty.

But it was on a social level that Victoria Eugenia made most impact on Spanish life. Court protocol was relaxed and women were no longer expected to wear the traditional clothes of mourning for years on end. Bright colours replaced black, as Madrid became a centre of fashion and design, capable of competing with the great fashion houses of Paris and Milan. In short, she brought the Spanish Court into the 20th century.

Unfortunately, in the political sphere Spain was still stuck in the past. Infighting between political factions and hastily contrived coalitions were commonplace and the constant interference of King Alfonso in political affairs caused even further instability. There were 33 different Governments between 1902 and 1923. In that year, Alfonso virtually endorsed General Primo de Rivera's "temporary" dictatorship, a decision which was to fan the fire of Republicanism and anti-monarchist feeling.

As Primo de Rivera's regime continued and discontent mounted, Alfonso was increasingly seen as an irresponsible playboy isolated from reality. Unrest among students surprised him, since he had tried to conciliate them by taking a personal interest in Madrid's University City. But

Facing page: Princess Victoria Eugenia of Battenberg, the favourite grand-daughter of Queen Victoria, who married the young Spanish King Alfonso XIII.

because of his support for the dictatorship, his statue was vandalised and special police squads were deployed to remove seditious graffiti.

Alfonso continued his taste for shooting and polo in the company of aristocratic courtiers, but when Primo de Rivera resigned in 1930, the monarchy's days were numbered. When the inevitable end came, Alfonso airily remarked to Queen

Facing page: Queen Victoria Eugenia with the Duchesss of Aosta during a visit to Naples in 1923. Above: King Alfonso XIII riding on the Duke of Sutherland's estate in Scotland.

Above: the Queen leaving her hotel in Paris during her exile to do some shopping and, right: waving goodbye at Madrid airport in February 1968 at the end of her only visit to Spain since being exiled.

Ena: "We are out of fashion", while his polo coach, the Marques de Villavieja, described it as "a greater shock then any fall from a polo pony."

In April 1931, municipal elections throughout Spain became a test case for the monarchy itself. 46 of 50 provincial capitals went Republican, a result that meant the finish of the Bourbon dynasty that had ruled for over two centuries. Acknowledging that he no longer enjoyed sufficient support from the Spanish people, Alfonso left for Paris and exile. A few days later, he was followed by his wife Victoria Eugenia. Queen Ena was to remain in exile for the rest of her life, dying in Switzerland in 1969.

Above: at her burial in the Sacred Heart Church at Ouchy, Lausanne, Switzerland, in April 1969, Victoria Eugenia´s coffin is lowered into the grave by members of the Spanish Royal family. In the foreground, the young Prince of Asturias, later to become the present King of Spain, Juan Carlos I.

POSIBLE SITUACION ECONÓMICA DE NUESTROS NIETOS

RESUMEN DE LA CONFERENCIA ORGANIZADA POR EL COMITÉ HISPANO-INGLÉS,
Y DADA EN LA RESIDENCIA DE ESTUDIANTES EL DÍA 10 DE JUNIO DE 1930

POR

J. M. KEYNES

I

Nosotros, en Inglaterra, estamos pasando por una época de fuerte pesimismo en materia económica. No sé si ustedes, los españoles, tienen la misma preocupación. Es posible que sí.

En Inglaterra se dice corrientemente que la época del gran progreso económico, característico del siglo XIX, ha pasado ya; que el aumento rápido del tipo (standard) de vida llevará desde ahora un ritmo más lento; que es más probable decrezca la prosperidad, en lugar de aumentar, durante el decenio en que entramos.

A mi juicio, los que así opinan, dan una interpretación completamente equivocada a lo que nos sucede a nosotros, y al resto del mundo. Estamos sufriendo, no de los achaques de la vejez, sino de las molestias naturales originadas por cambios demasiado bruscos y

J. M. Keynes. (Fot. del film de la R.)

lo doloroso que es el reajuste entre uno y otro período económico. El rendimiento técnico ha ido aumentando más rápidamente que nuestra capacidad para absorber el sobrante de la mano de obra; el bienestar general ha crecido con prisa algo excesiva.

Todos sufrimos—España, creo, tanto como los demás países—de la depresión cíclica actual. Esto nos impide ver lo que está sucediendo en el fondo, y dar con la verdadera interpretación del mundo en que vivimos.

Porque yo creo que nadie ha de quedar tan en ridículo, dentro de unos años, como esos agoreros pesimistas. Ambos opuestos pesimismos, que hoy día arman tanto ruido en el mundo, resultarán equivocados; el pesimismo de los revolucionarios, viéndolo todo tan mal que no hay otro remedio que un cambio violento, y el de los reaccionarios al estimar tan precario el equilibrio de nuestra actual vida económica y social, que todo nuevo experimento sería arriesgado.

Sin embargo, mi objeto en esta conferencia no es tanto examinar el momento presente como, prescindiendo de perspectivas limitadas, dejar a la imaginación tomar vuelo hacia el futuro. ¿Cuál ha de ser, lógicamente pensando, el nivel de nuestra vida económica dentro de cien años? ¿Cuáles han de ser las posibilidades económicas que aguardan a nuestros nietos?

Desde los tiempos más remotos de que poseemos datos—aproximadamente desde 2.000 años antes de J. C. hasta principios del siglo XVIII—, no hubo gran cambio en las condiciones materiales de la vida del hombre normal en los centros civilizados de la tierra. Vicisitudes las hubo. Catástrofes de pestes, hambres, guerras, con áureos intervalos. Pero sin cambios progresivos ni violentos. Algunas épocas, quizás un cincuenta por ciento, a lo sumo un cien por ciento, mejores que otras, durante los cuatro mil años que terminaron alrededor del 1700 de nuestra era.

Esta lentitud o ausencia de progreso obedecía a dos causas: a la falta notable de importantes perfeccionamientos técnicos y a la ausencia del capital acumulado. La carencia de inventos técnicos de importancia entre la edad prehistórica y los tiempos relativamente modernos, es muy notable. Casi todo lo que importa y que poseía el mundo al empezar la moderna era, ya lo conocía el hombre en la aurora de la historia. El lenguaje, el fuego, los animales domésticos de hoy, el trigo, la cebada, la vid y el olivo, el arado, la rueda, el remo, la vela, el cuero, los tejidos de lino y lana, los ladrillos y la cerámica, el oro y la plata; el cobre, el estaño y el plomo, las instituciones bancarias, la religión, el arte político, la matemática, la astronomía, no hay noticia concreta que indique cuándo el hombre entró en posesión de todo ello.

15

Chapter VIII
Illustrious Visitors
Residencia de Estudiantes in Madrid

An offspring of the Institución Libre de Enseñanza (Free Teaching Institution) founded in1876, the Residencia de Estudiantes – often abbreviated to "Resi" – was founded in 1910 to provide a hostel, with tutorial services, for students at Madrid University. The demand for places was so great that it was expanded to accommodate 150 students.

The young warden, Alberto Jiménez Fraud, had taught at the Institución Libre and was inspired by its liberal idealism. Convinced that Spain's intellectual progress depended on the creation of a carefully nurtured elite, he had also shown a close interest in the college system at Oxford and Cambridge Universities and had visited England to study it.

Fraud wanted to bridge the gap between the sciences and the humanities so that students would have a more balanced education. He was in fact a missionary, striving for a new Spain more open to ideas, and hoped that the Residencia would produce students with similar ideals. Among them in the 1920s were the poet Federico García Lorca, the artist Salvador Dalí and the film-maker Luis Buñuel.

As part of the mind-broadening programme, many distinguished people, Spanish and foreign, were invited to lecture at the Residencia which rapidly became one of the most vibrant intellectual centres in Europe. Guest speakers included Albert Einstein, Marie Curie, the architect Le Corbusier and the philosopher Henri Bergson. Among British speakers were H. G. Wells, G. K. Chesterton, Hilaire Belloc, the economist John Maynard Keynes, the archaeologists Howard Carter and Sir Leonard Woolley, the scientist Sir Arthur Eddington and the architect Sir Edwin Lutyens.

Musicians, among them the New English Singers, gave concerts, and leading composers and musical critics came to the "Resi". J. B. Trend, an English musicologist, later Professor of Spanish at Cambridge University, was a visiting lecturer who saw how greatly its methods and informal atmosphere had been influenced by English models, in particular the tutorial system. It was, he wrote, "Oxford and Cambridge in Madrid", and the aim was "to awaken curiosity – a faculty lacking in many Spaniards, and to arouse the power to make personal judgements instead of accepting what other people say." He

Facing page: a report in the Madrid magazine "Residencia" on a conference given at the Residencia de Estudiantes by the British economist John Maynard Keynes.

noted that the Residencia was beginning to publish books, in the manner of British university presses.

Another unmistakable sign of British influence was the *mens sana in corpore sano* (a healthy mind in a healthy body) emphasis on the importance of physical exercise. There were facilities for football, tennis, hockey and athletics – sporty ingredients of the prevailing ideal of "balance". Alcohol was forbidden, while the constant tea drinking in students' rooms (sparsely furnished as at Oxbridge) was a further example of adoption of British customs. J.B. Trend was also impressed with the Residencia's extensive library of modern publications which, as at Oxbridge, students could use to browse or borrow. This freedom, he said, was in startling contrast to his research experience at other Spanish libraries, where one might not even be allowed see the catalogue.

The Residencia's modernising, internationally minded and essentially secular regime was bound to stir controversy and opposition. General Miguel Primo de Rivera's right-wing coup in 1923 had repercussions at the Residencia that, for a while, struggled to survive unscathed. In 1936, the coming of the Civil War closed down the Residencia, and not until 1986 did it fully re-open and become once again a thriving centre of cultural interchange.

Now a private foundation with the Spanish Minister of Education as President, it has once more featured many guest speakers under the auspices of the British Hispanic Foundation and the British Council. Lecturers have included the historian Sir Raymond Carr, the scientist Roger

The Residencia de Estudiantes in Madrid, a meeting place during the inter-war years for intellectuals and artists from all over the world.

Above left: guest speaker H.G. Wells, who spoke on "Money and Mankind" at the Residencia in 1932. *Above right:* General C.G. Bruce, who gave a talk in 1926 entitled "Climbing Everest". *Facing page:* G.K. Chesterton and his wife in Madrid in 1926. The British writer lectured twice at the Residencia.

Penrose, the novelists David Lodge, Malcolm Bradbury, John Berger and William Boyd and the poet David Gascoyne. Members of the Royal Shakespeare Company and musicians such as the London Consort have performed at the Residencia, and Britons are among the 3000 students and researchers who each year use its extensive archives.

Chapter IV

The Spanish Attraction
Writers Who Stayed and Stayed

For romantic and escapist British intellectuals, Spain in the 1920s had a strong fascination. Neutral during the Great War, it was to them, as to Richard Ford, a land full of archaic surprises. In 1920 Osbert Sitwell was thrilled at the Pyrenean frontier by huge, towering clouds, dramatic shafts of sunlight, "women carrying pitchers to the wells, men with straw hats as big as wheels, hogskins filled with wine…All possessed the indefinable tang of an ancient and historic country."

Among the literary pilgrims of that period were the hard-up writers V. S. Pritchett and Laurie Lee. In 1925, Pritchett walked from Badajoz to León and before that, as correspondent of the Christian Science Monitor, had remarked on the leisurely pace of travel in Spain. The train journey from the French border to Madrid took 18 hours. Surfaced roads were rare and often so bad that cars seldom used them. Goats were driven to market through the streets of Madrid, which "was packed with Government employees, most of them obliged to do two or three jobs to stay alive. Delay was the only serious labour."

The young poet Laurie Lee, who tramped down Spain in 1935-36 with his fiddle and boyish charm, recreated the experience over 30 years later in the lushly lyrical *As I Walked Out One Midsummer Morning*. The landscapes of Spain inspired in him such paeans as had not been written since the then aspiring young writer Benjamin Disraeli had in 1830 enthused in Andalucía "Oh Wonderful Spain! Think of this romantic land covered with Moorish ruins and full of Murillo!"

Lee's images cascade. "Great gold plains, where the sun rose up like a butcher each morning and left curtains of blood each night." Cádiz is "a scribble of white on a sheet of blue glass". The town of Toro looks "like dried blood on a rusty sword." But nearing Málaga he describes "a beautiful but exhausted shore…San Pedro, Estepona, Marbella and Fuengirola…salt-fish villages, thin-ribbed, sea-hating, cursing their place in the sun."

His book *A Rose In Winter*, evoking some months spent in Andalucía in 1950-51, captures the vibrance beneath the gloomy surface of a country deeply ravaged by civil war. According

Facing page: Robert Graves, the English poet who arrived in Mallorca in 1929 and was treated like a local squire in the fishing village of Deya where he made his home.

to Lee, gypsies are "one of the aristocracies of Spain: indolent, insolent, rapacious and admired. They have annexed the folklore of the country which they exploit with a brilliant and swashbuckling technique." And he listens to the bawdy kitchen gossip of women "discussing love, murder, the price of meat, the fatness of Franco and the parts of their men."

But the two long-term British expatriates inseparably associated with Spain are Gerald Brenan and Robert Graves. During the six years he spent between 1920 and 1934 in Yegen, a rather ugly village high in the Alpujarra, Brenan, ultimately to be celebrated as the author of such enduring classics as *South from Granada*, *The Spanish Labyrinth*, *The Literature of the Spanish People* and *The Face of Spain*, was engaged in a marathon of self-education. Like Robert Graves, he fled from an England dominated by

stuffy public school values and from horrific memories of murderous trench warfare in the First World War. Neither he nor Graves had any particular interest in Spain or its culture. Brenan sought a remote, cheap retreat where, with a library of some 2000 books bought and transported with his officer's gratuity, he could indulge an insatiable intellectual curiosity.

Facing page: Gerald Brenan as a young man in Yegen in 1922 and, above, dining al fresco in his village home in Churriana near Málaga in 1959 with his wife Gamel, left, and Ernest Hemingway.

His friend V. S. Pritchett described Brenan as "an encyclopaedia with wings" and to the illiterate villagers this shy, lanky stranger was an object of exotic peculiarity. Such was the isolation from the world outside Yegen that he was thought to have been fighting against the Moors. Apart from a brief sexual liaison with a village girl, and some brothel visits in Seville and Almería, Brenan's social contacts were mainly with his British friends. Lytton Strachey, Dora Carrington, Virginia Woolf, Bertrand Russell and Augustus John all visited and corresponded with this mature student, living on a grudging allowance from his father, who got nothing published until the age of 40. When he married it was to an American poet, Gamel Woolsey.

Yet *South from Granada*, published in 1957 when the Brenans were living in the village of Churriana near Málaga, displayed a minute knowledge of the folklore and social nuances of Yegen and its environs. A respected figure in literary and academic circles, Brenan in old age suddenly, to his bewilderment, became a celebrity in Spain. Virtually kidnapped from an old people's home in London in 1984, aged 90 and half-blind, he was flown back to Spain, facing a barrage of TV cameras and jostling journalists. In his house in Alhaurín el Grande near Churriana, the municipality paid for round-the-clock nursing care for this cultural icon whose vestigial presence attracted visitors and interviewers from all over the world. He died in 1987.

Robert Graves, already well known as a poet and soon to be famous as the author of *Goodbye to All That*, arrived in Majorca in 1929. Resolved "never to make England my home again", he found in Deya, then a small fishing village, the haven he desired. Here, at least temporarily, was a paradise for technophobes, where "country was country…and the horse plough not yet an anachronism", labour was incredibly cheap and Graves, though far from rich and the centre of a bickering literary clique, was given local squire status.

Just as erudite in his occultist way as Brenan, he was almost equally remote from local concerns. Unlike the Dublin-born Hispanist Ian Gibson who took Spanish nationality and writes, lectures and broadcasts in Spanish, Graves wrote very little about Spain, all his major works, including *I, Claudius* and *The White Goddess*, having non-Spanish themes. His poems inspired by non-Spanish muse-mistresses, were little known in Majorca. Yet with his much-publicised affairs, ruggedly handsome looks, and lecture tours in England and America, Graves was a "Spanish" celebrity to the international media long before Brenan's belated apotheosis.

The writings of Laurie Lee, Graves and even the donnish Brenan, helped to bring a new wave of tourism and expatriate escapism which all three were to deplore.

Facing page: English poet Laurie Lee, during one of his last visits to southern Spain in 1993. *Above:* the poet as a young man in southern Spain.

Chapter X

The Idealists

British Volunteers Who Fought in Spain

Some saw the Spanish Civil War (1936-39) as "The Last Great Cause". The British Foreign Secretary, Sir Anthony Eden, worried by the possible repercussions of foreign intervention, called it "The War of the Spanish Obsession". The Government tried to prevent British volunteers from leaving the country to join the Communist-organised International Brigades or other fighting units by making this illegal. But despite the efforts of the police, most of the volunteers reached Spain.

Because it sounded more idealistic than urging recruits to fight to establish a Communist regime, the British Communist Party preferred the slogan "Volunteers for Liberty." The Soviet line, approved by Stalin, was that military aid to Republican Spain was given not to make revolution but to defend a democratic government from Fascist attack.

The first British casualty was a woman, Felicia Browne, an artist who happened to be in Barcelona for the Workers' Olympiad, an alternative to the "Hitler Olympics" in Berlin. She joined one of the fairly chaotic Republican militia columns and died on the 25 August 1936 during an attempt to blow up a railway station. The very first English volunteers were two London tailors, communists like Felicia Browne, who were on a cycling holiday in France and crossed the border to do their bit in Barcelona.

British volunteers for the International Brigades, at first scattered in various units, fought in the fierce battles around Madrid. One group — almost wiped out at Boadilla — included the non-Communist Esmond Romilly, a rebellious 18-year-old nephew of Winston Churchill, fresh from public school, Romilly began by treating the conflict as a high-spirited lark, but soon realised that the Germans he fought alongside, all fugitives from Nazi terror, were in deadly earnest. Like Italian political refugees, they had no home to return to. For them the Spanish War was a chance to strike back.

There was no lack of political consciousness among the British volunteers who were formed into their own Battalion in February 1937. About 80% were of working class origin, often unemployed during the Depression. Yet the great majority, including the unemployed, had decided that to fight Fascism was a moral duty. Ignorant of the

Facing page: one of the many British woman volunteers who fought in the Spanish Civil War or worked as nurses.

Spanish political labyrinth, they mingled sympathy with the Republican underdogs with loathing for their oppressors. A Welsh volunteer, in a letter to a friend, wrote that "the poor class of Spain are 500 years behind time…they have been kept under like dogs, but the people have risen now.'

26-year-old Frank Deegan was a fairly typical volunteer. An out-of-work Liverpool docker and a Communist, he "believed the international rich ruling class had ganged up to help Franco defeat a legally elected people's government." At a daily wage of 10 pesetas (about two shillings at that time), Brigaders could hardly be called "Red mercenaries", though there were some adventurers who found the going too tough and deserted.

By 1938, conditions were desperate in the battered British battalion. Out of around 2000 volunteers, 500 were killed and 1,200 wounded . "Often we had only canvas shoes or wrapped rags around our feet…we tried everything to get a smoke…the best were sun-dried potato leaves, almost like real tobacco."

Frank Deegan remembers that before the final decisive battle of the Ebro (July-November 1938), faced by overwhelming Nationalist superiority in artillery and air power, they had a good sing-song: "Hitler and Franco your future looks black / Workers battalions are driving you back / Sons of the masses forever we be / Forward ye toilers to victory…'"

But pinned down in scorching heat under incessant bombardment, they asked themselves "is this goddam piece of real estate worth fighting for?" Deegan, at that time working as a stretcher-bearer, carrying some of his best friends dead, dying or badly wounded, was himself lacerated by a bursting grenade late in September. After hospital treatment in Barcelona, he returned to Liverpool and, like other ex-International Brigaders, was regarded by employers as a potential trouble maker.

Above: a volunteer in the British Battalion, photographed
in 1937 with Spanish boy Anastasio Mariscal.

The sometimes naïve idealism of many volunteers was cynically manipulated as the beleaguered Republic was increasingly rent by ideological disagreements, revolving around resentment at Soviet control and the feeling among Anarchists and radical Socialists that the war was not worth fighting unless it aimed at a thoroughgoing social revolution.

Above: John Cornford, the young English poet recently graduated from Cambridge, who was killed in action near Córdoba in December 1936.

This passion for a social revolution had caused 20-year-old John Cornford, a poet and keen communist recently graduated from Cambridge, to join one of the many militias that sprouted early in the war. He had been captivated by the romantic idealism and comradeship of the Spanish Anarchists. He was killed in action near Córdoba in December, 1936.

In his masterpiece *Homage to Catalonia*, George Orwell gave the first, and still classic, account of the civil-war-within-the-civil-war in Spain. Rejected by the International Brigades and suspicious of Russian intentions, he eventually joined the militia of the anti-Stalinist POUM (Workers Party of Marxist Unity) on the stagnant Aragon front. Bored soldiers sniped at each other from the trenches or exchanged megaphone insults. For Orwell, an Old Etonian who had served in the Indian Imperial Police before exploring the hobo underworld in Paris and London, it was an eye opening experience. Many militiamen were illiterate teenagers who had enlisted for the pittance pay and miserable food. Rifles were antiquated 1894 Mausers. Elected a cabo (corporal), he was accused of behaving like a fascist when he tried to enforce obedience to an order.

The tedium of the trenches was enlivened by frequent debates on war aims. Still formulating his own socialist ideals, Orwell, a tall, gaunt, outlandish intellectual with size 12 boots and a complete disregard for his safety, listened carefully, frequently consulting a pocket Spanish dictionary. By the time he was shot through the throat in June 1937, never having bothered to keep his head down, he was convinced that, as a POUM slogan put it, "the war and the revolution are inseparable", that arms had been deliberately withheld from the Aragon front "lest Anarchists should use them for a revolutionary purpose", thus preventing a much-needed offensive, and that the Communist aim was "not to postpone the Spanish revolution but to make sure that it never happened."

He had noticed the contrast between sleek, well-armed police in Barcelona and the ragged, ill-equipped militia at the front. His conclusions were startlingly confirmed when, emerging from hospital and accompanied by his wife Eileen, he was caught up in an anti-POUM pogrom and barely avoided arrest and imprisonment as a "fascist".

Back in England Orwell, like Deegan, found himself an object of suspicion, but for different reasons. His publishers thought him an anti-Communist crank, and he had to struggle to get his reportage printed. But he was grateful to his comrades in Aragon for completing his political education. "The Spanish war," he wrote, "turned the scale…Every line of serious work I have written since then has been…against totalitarianism and for democratic socialism as I understand it." His book *"Animal Farm"* (1945), the most powerful parable of modern times, was rooted in the squalid trenches of Aragón and the murderous dirty war in Barcelona.

Above: George Orwell standing head and shoulders above the rest of the soldiers during machine gun practice at the Aragón front in 1937.

AL
Dr FLEMING
EN AGRADECIMIENTO
DE LOS TOREROS
14 MAYO 1964

Chapter XI
Sir Alexander Fleming
Bullfighters Pay Homage to a Scotsman

On returning from holiday to his laboratory at St. Mary´s Hospital in London in 1928, the Scottish bacteriologist Alexander Fleming discovered that the bacterial culture he had left in a petri dish had grown a "blue mould" that inhibited bacterial growth. He had discovered penicillin, arguably one of the most important events of the 20th century.

As the first-ever antibiotic drug, it was used to treat wounded soldiers during the Second World War, and since 1940 it is estimated to have saved literally millions of lives.

In Spain, bullfighters had reason to be particularly grateful to Fleming's discovery. Before the introduction of penicillin, doctors had been unable to prevent infection setting in whatever the severity of a wound. Often the matadors would die from relatively minor gorings because the tissue became infected. Penicillin considerably increased life expectancy among toreros. The statue erected outside Madrid's famous bullring, Las Ventas, expresses their gratitude to Dr Fleming.

In fact, Spain had already paid tribute to him. At the end of May 1948, Fleming had arrived at Barcelona for a triumphal tour. Knighted in 1944 and a Nobel Prize winner in 1945, he had become a world hero. Honours had been showered upon him in the USA, Scandinavia, France, Belgium and Italy; yet he liked to describe himself as "a simple laboratory worker who played with microbes."

In Barcelona, while Fleming walked in a mayoral procession along the Rambla de las Flores, the flower sellers threw roses and carnations on the ground in front of him. There followed ten days, and banqueted nights, of receptions, presentations, galas and ceremonies. He gave several lectures, unveiled a stone commemorating his visit, and received various honours. He and his wife Sareen were entertained to lunch at the monastery of Montserrat, and found it a more relaxing occasion. The meal was eaten in complete silence, much appreciated after so many compulsorily talkative repasts.

Sir Alexander Fleming's tour of Andalusia included Seville, Córdoba, and Jerez de la Frontera. At Jerez, after being shown the huge bodega casks signed by Nelson, Wellington and Pitt, he was invited to sign one himself. Having

Facing page: a torero outside Las Ventas bullring in Madrid, in 1964, saluting the statue of the Scottish bacteriologist Alexander Fleming.

Above: Dr. Fleming being welcomed by the Mayor of Madrid on his arrival at Barajas airport in June 1948.

done so, he remarked that his signature was more legible because "he had been taught to write in Scotland!"

The schedule of Fleming's Madrid visit, starting on 11 June, was exhaustingly strenuous, as after a day of speeches and ceremonies he hurried back to his hotel suite to change clothes for yet another gala or ball. He was invested with the regalia of a Doctorate of Natural Science and with the sash and Grand Cross of the order of

Alfonso X. The eminent physician and writer Dr Gregorio Marañón commented that "God selected him to carry out the greatest miracle which humanity has ever seen."

When Fleming died aged 74 on 11 April 1955, the flower sellers in Barcelona laid bunches of roses and carnations at the foot of the stone marking his 1948 visit. Dr Marañón solemnly announced: "We can be sure that at this moment he is sitting on the right hand of God the Father."

Above: Sir Alexander Fleming being named "Dr. Honoris Causa" at Madrid University on 12 June 1948.

Chapter XII

David Lean

And the Almería Movie Boom

The English film director David Lean's epic masterpiece *Lawrence of Arabia*, nearly two years in the making, was beset with initial problems. The script had to be re-written. Marlon Brando turned down the lead role, so did Albert Finney. But when released in 1962, the film won an Oscar for Lean and made the young actor Peter O'Toole into a star.

Filmed in Jordan, Spain and Morocco, *Lawrence of Arabia* involved a demanding military-type operation. Working in desert or semi-desert terrain, a 400-strong team of actors, technicians and production staff needed a catering corps to feed them, accompanied by sleeping tents, equipment trucks, horse and camel handlers, plus vast quantities of food and water for the livestock.

After filming in Jordan from May 1961, the unit reassembled in Spain, where part of Seville doubled for Cairo, Damascus and Jerusalem, and many interior scenes were shot. But the most spectacular sequences were staged around Almería. Production headquarters were established in the city's bus station, and a 150-metre tramway was constructed in the Parque Nicolás Salmerón and the Parque José Antonio for Cairo scenes that were intercut with those filmed in Seville.

Over 400 horses were brought in from Jerez de la Frontera, Guadix, Seville and Madrid, while 150 camels were assembled from Morocco and various parts of Spain for the Aqaba episode. This required an elaborate reconstruction of the town that kept 200 locally recruited workers busy for three months. Built at Carboneras in a dried-up river bed on the Algarrobico beach, this remarkable set was in fact a cunning illusion, a series of carefully positioned facades that could only be filmed from one angle. Yet it represented an entire town, including a mosque and official buildings. Nearby was a Turkish camp with more than seventy tents, and several hundred Turkish soldiers took part in the defence of Aqaba. Most of the villagers of Carboneras were employed as extras.

In Cabo de Gata, sixty workers laid a 2.5 km railway track along which some 130,000 square metres of desert-simulating sand (raked smooth after each take) was shifted for the famous scene of the Arab attack on a Turkish train, led by a sword-brandishing Colonel Lawrence. The loco-

Facing page: the British director David Lean, centre, who filmed some of the most famous scenes of "Lawrence of Arabia" in the Almería desert and Seville, with Robert Bolt, left, who wrote the screen play, and Eddie Fowlie, who found the locations in Spain for the film.

motive was transported in sections to the location by lorry. An international array of TV camera crews was on hand to cover this all-action sequence, but because of the danger to horses and extras it was decided not, as originally intended, to blow up the train. Instead it was derailed.

Other villages featuring in the film were El Alquián, Gergal, Níjar and Rodalquilar. When the unit moved onto Morocco, the "oasis" created near the village of Tabernas with palm trees from

Above: A film set built in the desert, behind Almería where the making of "Lawrence of Arabia" started a film boom in the sixties.

Alicante, remained — and is still there as a souvenir of the four hectic months when David Lean and his associates put Almería on the movie-making map. The actor Anthony Quinn is fondly remembered at the Los Cármenes del Zapillo bar, which he and his double frequented, and Eddie Fowlie, who constructed the oasis, stayed on to become proprietor of the El Dorado Hotel in Carboneras.

David Lean came back to Spain, but this time to Madrid and around Soria, to make "*Dr Zhivago*" (1965) and was about to return to Almería as the setting for an adaptation of Joseph Conrad's novel "*Nostromo*" when he died in April 1991.

After Lawrence of Arabia had blazed the trail, other film makers were drawn to Almería. During the 1960s Clint Eastwood, Lee Van Cleef, Charles Bronson, Brigitte Bardot and Raquel Welch, among others, were at work in the vicinity.

As many as nine films were in production at the same time and Sergio Leone directed his well-known spaghetti westerns *The Good, the Bad and the Ugly* and *A Fistful of Dollars* here.

The sun, brilliant light, an arid landscape resembling the Wild West of Arizona, and low labour costs kept the boom going for several years, but it eventually came to an end as production costs began to rise in Almería and other, cheaper locations were found.

At Tabernas or "Mini Hollywood", a replica Wild West town where more than 100 films were made, some Spanish veterans of those days still appear in a few movies and TV commercials, but mostly they performed for coachloads of package tourists, staging hold-ups and gunfights, or posing for photographs.

The fastidious, gentlemanly David Lean may have found this mass production sequel to his classy epic rather tatty, but it kept much needed cash flowing into Almería until the 1970s. Its demise left a hole in the local economy that was ultimately filled by the amazing "plasticultura" boom of fruit, vegetables and flowers mass-produced under vast plastic tents.

Above: one of the many spaghetti westerns filmed in the Almería desert.

Chapter XIII

A Genteel Invasion
Then the Assault on the Costas

In the 1890s, Alfred L. Jones, a long-standing resident of Las Palmas, persuaded shipping companies to reduce fares from Liverpool, and with the resulting increase of British tourists to the Canary Islands, local businesses and hotels prospered. Jones's initiative is one of the earliest examples of cut-price holidays designed to attract Britons to Spain.

In those days, British tourism was distinctly genteel compared to the frenetic "sex, sun, sand and sangria" mass tourism which took shape on the Spanish mainland in the 1960s. At first, Britons came to the Canaries to reap the beneficial effects of the climate. Long walks along the beaches, an occasional dip in the bracing Atlantic Ocean, then afternoon tea on the hotel terrace. Quiet and repose were the order of the day.

On the Peninsula itself, British tourism was largely confined to passengers from the cruise ships which docked in Barcelona en route to other Mediterranean destinations, and to Thomas Cook's select groups who would visit the cities with the most important cultural attractions such as Madrid, Toledo, Granada and Seville.

Until well into the 20th century, the British tourist was still a rarity. In *"Fabled Shore"*, Rose Macaulay commented that while driving south in Spain in 1947 she "encountered hardly any travelling compatriots and saw only one GB car". But in 1958, visa restrictions on foreigners were lifted and this measure, combined with a north European economic surge, began to put a holiday in Spain within the reach of less well-to-do British households. The traditional British holiday of amusement arcades, shingly beaches and strolls along the pier had to compete with the sandy beaches of the Spanish Costas.

In 1901, Baedeker's Guide had warned that "the climatic advantages of such places as Alicante, Almería and Málaga are largely counterbalanced by their dirt, dust and general lack of comforts. An increase in the number of foreign visitors is the surest way to bring about a change for the better." And just as Britons had led the way in the railway tourism of the 19th century, so they did in the jet plane package holiday boom which, as Gerald Brenan remarked, "has changed the face of Spain almost beyond recognition."

Particularly so in Majorca, the Costa Brava and the Costa del Sol, which in 1936 Laurie Lee had

Facing page: an elegant British tourist poses on a camel during a holiday in the 1880´s in Puerto de la Luz in the Canary Islands.

Above: British tourists disembarking from the ship Alcántara in 1928 in Barcelona.

described as "cursing its place in the sun". By the late 1980s, the Costa del Sol had more tourist beds than all of Greece. Tourist figures had risen from 1 million from 1968 in to more than 5 million, one-third of foreign arrivals being British.

Change was bewilderingly rapid. In 1935, when Nancy and Archie Johnstone opened the first foreign-run hotel on the Costa Brava at Tossa del Mar, self-conscious, amply covered Britons on the beach with their lilos were watched with amusement by the locals. By 1954, Tossa boasted 32 hotels with more to come.

Within a decade or so Torremolinos, once favoured by artists and eccentric hell-raisers, became a mass tourist destination, one of the "Golden Ghettos" that aimed to corral cut-price sun-and-fun seekers in faintly Spanish homes-from-home. In Majorca, Robert Graves was in 1965 alarmed by "the brand-new phenomenon of mass tourism, meaning char-

Above: the British ocean liner Otranto and, at left, the yacht Dolphin used by Neville Chamberlain, both photographed in 1927 in the Port of Barcelona.

ter flights, block-booking of hotels and so clever a rationalisation of ways and means that a fortnight's vacation would cost no more than an individual return fare." The result was 5000 flights a month in summer to an ever-expanding Palma airport. He disliked "flamenco-strumming by pretended gypsies," and deplored the neglect of agriculture – so that "at Deya we now import gypsies from Andalucía, at huge expense to get in the olive harvest."

Other Britons who had known Spain between the wars were similarly dismayed. Brenan saw that mass tourism had brought with it the mass

Facing page: a well-groomed British tourist takes a snapshot during a visit to Madrid in 1965.
Above: the Duke and Duchess of Kent during their stay at Hotel Taoro in Tenerife in 1938.

Above: a pipe-smoking British tourist and his lady sporting a parasol stroll along a Formentor beach in Mallorca in the 1920's

culture of TV and the transistor radio, so that the intense pride of place shown in such *coplas* as *Sanlúcar de Barrameda / Would I could carry you folded in my pocket like a piece of paper* was vanishing. Laurie Lee, once optimistic that the "true Spain would somehow survive the tourist deluge," decided that it had been a total disaster. "The culture has been crippled," he said.

Writing of a 1961 horseback trek through the Sierra de Cazorla, Penelope Chetwode, pleased to find villages much the same as in the days of Ford and Borrow, frowned upon such novelties as radios blaring bad flamenco music, plastic

crockery and the flight of young men to the coast to service the tourist trade.

But in *The Presence of Spain* (1964) James Morris, a newcomer to the scene, argued that there was much to applaud in the consequences of this astonishing "mass migration of people to a single destination – and this to the most resolutely insular state in Europe." The tourist invasion, which in the 1890s Havelock Ellis had seen as nibbling at the roots of Spanish cultures yet, at the same time, forcing an improvement in hygiene, had by the 1970s comprehensively breached the defences of Franco's primly repressive regime.

Above: a Mallorcan cove, where the favourite activities for tourists during the 1920´s were bathing in the sea and going for long walks along the beach before taking tea on the hotel terrace.

Above: bikini-clad English tourists cycling through the centre of a Costa del Sol resort in the early 1960´s. *Facing page*: bemused locals watch as two English tourists walk down a cobbled street in Torremolinos in 1965.

An ailing economy had been massively boosted, democracy had been smuggled into Spain with the bikinis and the sexually liberated ways of young British women on the spree, and it would not be long before Spanish women cast off their Moorish shackles and machismo came under fire. On the costas a social revolution had been unleashed with English as the *lingua franca*.

Spain's "difference", so cherished by romantic British writers, now meant fake-flamenco, dying villages, farming land sold to concrete jungle developers, ploughboys as waiters or gigolos, small shopkeepers turned supermarket tycoons. The question remained, said Morris: had the exchange of picturesque poverty for a socially mobile consumer society, spear-headed by British tourists and senior citizen expatriates, emasculated the sense of style that had been the essence of the Spanish Attraction?

Suggested Further Reading

Hugh Thomas, *The Spanish Civil War* (Penguin Books 1977)

Raymond Carr, *Spain 1807-1975* (OUP 1982)

Paul Preston, *Franco: A Biography* (Harper Collins 1993)

Ian Gibson, *Federico García Lorca: A Life* (Faber & Faber, 2000)

Michael Jacobs, *A Guide to Andalusia* (Viking 1990), *Between Hopes and Memories: A Spanish Journey* (Picador 1994)

David Mitchell, *Travellers in Spain* (Lookout Publications 1990), *The Spanish Civil War* (Granada Publishing 1982)

Jimmy Burns, *Spain: A Literary Companion* (John Murray 1994)

Robert Graves, *Majorca Observed* (Cassell 1965)

Jonathan Gathorne-Hardy, *The Interior Castle: A Life of Gerald Brenan* (Sinclair-Stevenson 1992)

John Hooper, *The New Spaniards* (Penguin Books 1995)

Ronald Fraser, *The Pueblo: A Mountain Village on the Costa del Sol* (Allen Lane 1973)

Nancy Johnstone, *Hotel in Spain* (Faber 1937)

Gerard Noel, *Ena: Spain's English Queen* (Constable 1990)

Julian Jeffs, *Sherry* (Faber & Faber 1992)

Julian Pitt-Rivers, *The People of the Sierra* (Weidenfeld & Nicolson 1954)

Norman Lewis, *Voices of the Old Sea* (Penguin 1985)

Louis Turner & John Ash, *The Golden Hordes: International Tourism and the Pleasure Periphery* (Constable 1975)

Havelock Ellis, *The Soul of Spain* (Constable 1908)

Helmut Gernsheim, *The History of Photography* (Thames & Hudson 1969)

For our full list of books on Spain,
send for our free catalogue:

Santana Books,

Apartado 422,
29640 Fuengirola (Málaga) Spain.
Tel: 952 485 838. Fax: 952 485 367

E-mail: santana@vnet.es